America THE Beautiful

ATLANTA

DAN LIEBMAN

Photographs by RON SHERMAN

FIREFLY BOOKS

A FIREFLY BOOK

Published by Firefly Books Ltd. 2013

First printing

Publisher Cataloging-in-Publication Data (U.S.)
Dan Liebman, Dan.
    Atlanta / Dan Liebman.
[96] p. : col. photos. ; cm.
Includes index.
Summary: A photographic tour of one of the most beautiful and vibrant
cities; includes both well known sights and hidden gems.
ISBN-13: 978-1-77085-254-9
1. Atlanta (Ga.) — Pictorial works. I. Title.
917.582310443 dc23   F294.A83L543 2013

Published in the United States by
Firefly Books (U.S.) Inc.
P.O. Box 1338, Ellicott Station
Buffalo, New York 14205

Published in Canada by
Firefly Books Ltd.
50 Staples Avenue, Unit 1
Richmond Hill, Ontario L4B 0A7

Cover and interior design: Kimberley Young

Printed in China

ATLANTA was founded in 1837 as a railway center, and the city's population and importance as a commercial hub quickly grew. Twenty-four years later, General William T. Sherman and his troops burned the city to the ground. But in the aftermath of the Civil War, Atlanta rose from the ashes, slowly making its recovery and ultimately becoming the capital of the new South.

Today, Atlanta offers a fascinating and photogenic mixture of the old and the new, from stately mansions of a bygone era to a stunningly dramatic skyline that reflects the city's significance as a major commercial center.

So much of what has evolved in Atlanta is reflected in its buildings and streetscapes. Martin Luther King preached his message of nonviolent civil rights here, and the church where he served as co-pastor is part of a thriving neighborhood. Margaret Mitchell wrote *Gone with the Wind* here – and the apartment where she wrote it, which she nicknamed "the dump," is open to the public. Coca-Cola was invented here. You can take a tour at the World of Coca-Cola – and you can also enjoy the magnificent parks and renowned cultural institutions that resulted from its founders' philanthropy.

Among Atlanta's treasures, and there are too many to name here, are Centennial Olympic Park with its famous fountain of rings, the fabulously ornate Fox Theatre, the enormous Georgia Aquarium, the acclaimed High Museum of Art, and the inspiring Martin Luther King, Jr., National Historic Site and the Jimmy Carter Presidential Library. But more than "places" make a great city. Atlanta has history, heart and soul – as well as great shopping, unique dining experiences, a festival that celebrates the delicate dogwood blossom, parks made for people, and the eclectic charms of its residential areas. And few cities are home to as many professional sports teams or outstanding universities as Atlanta. Add the fact that the city is blessed by a climate that's temperate, yet enjoys the changing seasons.

Atlanta offers abundant pleasures – southern charm in a modern metropolis. In the pages that follow, we provide a sampling of the city – its landmarks, architectural gems, urban oases, cultural and sports institutions, leafy streets and family attractions. We hope you'll enjoy your visit as you travel the pages of *America the Beautiful – Atlanta*.

Atlanta's vibrant Centennial Olympic Park neighborhood, once a run-down part of the city, was converted into a gathering spot during the 1996 Centennial Olympic Games. Following the Games, a large part of the park was redesigned for public use. Today, it hosts year-round entertainment, including festivals and the Independence Day concert and fireworks display. The park is home of the world's largest Olympic Ring fountain, with 250 water jets.

Springvale Park, in the Inman Park neighborhood, is one of Atlanta's smaller, and loveliest, green spaces. The historic park, restored using the original 1903 plans, is located in the area where the Battle of Atlanta took place.

OPPOSITE PAGE: The beloved Academy Award–winning movie, *Driving Miss Daisy*, was filmed on locations around the city. This home, in the leafy Druid Hills neighborhood, served as "Miss Daisy's House" during the film's time span, from the late 1940s to the early 1970s.

Atlanta is famous for its parks and its dogwood trees. Chastain Park, in the northern part of the city, is in glorious bloom in April, when the delicate blossoms are in full abundance.

Woodruff Park, named for Robert W. Woodruff, the prominent Atlanta citizen who introduced Coca-Cola to the world, is located in the heart of the city's financial and entertainment districts. Locals and visitors alike enjoy the urban park's abundant lawns, sculpture and fountains. Crowds gather here during lunchtime and for special events.

The 1910 Beaux Arts Herndon Home, in the city's Sweet Auburn Historic District, was the residence of Alonzo Franklin Herndon, who was born into slavery and went on to become Atlanta's first African American millionaire. The 1910 building was declared a National Historic Landmark and is now a museum, open to the public on Tuesdays and Thursdays.

Gracious homes, such as this one in Inman Park, reflect the city's rich history. Developed in the late 19th century, Inman Park was Atlanta's first planned residential suburb and home to many of the city's most prestigious citizens. Over the years the area became more of a middle-class neighborhood, with smaller homes on divided lots.

Joel Hurt was one of the city's most important early builders and the promoter of Inman Park. This is his mansion, among the most photographed of the area.

OPPOSITE PAGE: Inman Park's Beath-Dickey House dates back to 1890. This Queen Anne Victorian home is featured in many architectural guides. Early Inman Park residents included Coca-Cola founder Asa G. Candler and two former governors of Georgia.

The Wren's Nest is a 19th-century farmhouse that once belonged to Joel Chandler Harris, author of the beloved Uncle Remus and Brer Rabbit stories. Harris lived here from 1881 to 1908 and wrote many of his stories on the front porch. The Wren's Nest offers daily tours, and storytelling on Saturdays. The rambling Victorian house, designated a National Landmark, is named for a family of wrens that nested in the mailbox.

OPPOSITE PAGE: The meticulously restored Swan House offers a glimpse into the life of wealthy Atlantans in the 1920s and 1930s. Swan House was the estate of Edward Hamilton Inman. Built in 1928, it was named for the decorative swans found throughout the interior.

The Atlanta History Center, located in the city's Buckhead area, includes one of the country's largest history museums. Exhibits tell the story of the city from its earliest settlers to the present. The center features beautiful gardens and trails, and includes two historic homes – the Tullie Smith Farm and Swan House.

The opulent Fox Theatre, one of the city's most beloved landmarks, is located on Peachtree Street. The mosque-like structure was designed in the late 1920s as headquarters for the Shriners organization, but opened as a movie palace. A National Historic Landmark, the fully restored theater operates today as a venue for live entertainment.

In 1923, Robert Woodruff became president of the Coca-Cola Company. He served the company for more than 60 years, introducing the beverage to the world. Woodruff practiced a lifetime of philanthropy – much of it anonymously – and had a significant influence on the city's business, cultural and political life.

The Woodruff Arts Center, opened in 1968, honors its greatest benefactor, Robert Woodruff. The center is home to the Alliance Theatre, the High Museum of Art and the Grammy Award–winning Atlanta Symphony Orchestra, which plays at the spacious Symphony Hall.

CREATING COMMUNITY The Jews of Atlanta From 1845 to the Present

The William Breman Jewish Heritage and Holocaust Museum is dedicated to Jewish history. It includes exhibits on Jewish life in Georgia and has a permanent display on the Holocaust.

RIGHT: Callanwolde was the home of Coca-Cola Company heir Charles Howard Candler. The magnificent Gothic-Tudor style estate, completed in 1920, is located in the Druid Hills neighborhood and today serves as a fine arts center for city residents.

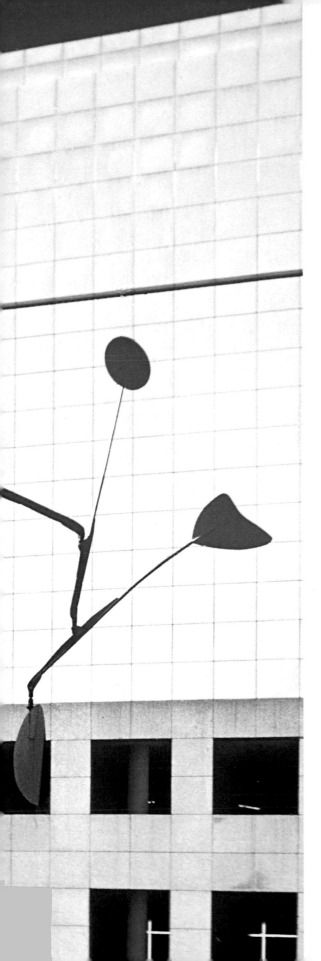

LEFT: The High Museum of Art, popularly called "the High," is the leading art museum in the Southeast and one of the most-visited art museums in the world. The High displays 19th- and 20th-century American art, European works and decorative art, African American art and folk art. The building itself is a work of art.

BELOW: The Apex (African American Panoramic Experience) Museum is a museum of history presented from the African American perspective. It is located on Auburn Avenue, in the city's Sweet Auburn historic district. The museum chronicles the history of the district and serves as a national African American cultural center.

The Fernbank Museum of Natural History brings to life the world's largest dinosaurs and invites visitors to explore the development of life on the planet. The museum's atrium features a 123-foot-long Argentinosaurus – the largest dinosaur ever classified.

The Michael C. Carlos Museum is located on the campus of Emory University in the city's Druid Hills area. Popular among both adults and children, it has a major collection of ancient art that includes objects from Egypt, Greece, Rome, the Near East, Africa and the ancient Americas.

ABOVE: Zoo Atlanta, one of the country's oldest zoos, is located in historic Grant Park. The zoo houses more than 1,500 animals representing over 200 species. It holds the largest collection of western lowland gorillas in North America and is one of only a few American zoos to house giant pandas.

LEFT: The Georgia Aquarium, located in downtown Atlanta, is the world's largest aquarium. It houses more than 100,000 animals, representing 500 species. Among the aquarium's specimens of marine life from around the world are whale sharks, beluga whales, penguins, bottlenose dolphins and manta rays.

The World of Coca-Cola presents a permanent exhibition featuring the history of the Coca-Cola Company. The museum houses a collection of Coca-Cola memorabilia, along with interactive displays. Every tour of the World of Coca-Cola concludes with a visit to "Taste It," where visitors enjoy free samples of more than 60 soft drinks from around the world. The statue is of John S. "Doc" Pemberton, the Atlanta pharmacist who invented Coke in 1886.

The CNN Center is the world headquarters of the Cable News Network. The main newsrooms and studios for several of CNN's news channels are located in the building. The CNN Studio Tour allows visitors the opportunity to visit newsrooms, tour a control room and see the network in action.

The Center for Puppetry Arts is a unique cultural experience. Home to a hands-on museum, the center has introduced millions of visitors to the wonder and art of puppetry. It presents performances, holds workshops and entertains and educates kids of all ages.

Imagine It! Children's Museum of Atlanta is a 30,000-square-foot complex located downtown, across the street from Centennial Olympic Park. It features activities that let kids discover how things work. The museum is recommended for children 2 to 8, but everyone is welcome.

At Legoland, kids of all ages learn Lego-building secrets from the master model builder. They also enjoy a tour of Atlanta's iconic landmarks – the fabulous Fox Theatre, the Georgia Aquarium, Stone Mountain Park and a great many more – all made out of plastic bricks.

The Atlanta Botanical Garden offers 30 acres
of exquisite gardens and conservatories.
It is well known for its Canopy Walk,
an interactive children's garden and the
Southern Seasons garden. Pictured here is
its distinguished orchid house – the Fuqua
Orchid Center – the largest in the country.

Downtown is the historic business district of the city and the largest of Atlanta's three commercial districts. (Midtown and Buckhead are the other two.) It is the location of many business and government facilities, sporting venues, and most of Atlanta's tourist attractions. SoNo (South of North Avenue) is a sub-district of Downtown.

The Cornerstone Building is a well-known Atlanta landmark, located at the corner of Peachtree Street and Andrew Young International Boulevard – the center of Downtown's hotel and convention district.

There is a profusion of color in Atlanta during the fall months. The city skyline makes a beautiful backdrop for this autumn scene.

Atlanta's skyline reflects the city's position as a center of commerce. The tall pinnacled tower is the Bank of America Plaza, Georgia's highest building – and the tallest building in any state capital. Designed in the Art Deco style, its spire is mostly covered in 23-karat gold. In the foreground is another gold-domed building, the Georgia State Capitol.

Piedmont Park, in Midtown Atlanta, is one of the city's favorite open spaces. A peaceful retreat of 185 acres, it is home to the Atlanta Botanical Garden. Since 1904, visitors have enjoyed its picnic spots, sports fields and walking paths. The park's green fields are well maintained, the lake includes several docks, and there are playgrounds and dog areas. Festivals and events take place throughout the year.

The 60-story SunTrust Plaza is part of the Peachtree Center and the tallest building in the Downtown area. (It is the second-tallest in the city.) The two-level lobby is filled with works of art and sculpture. Architect John Portman's sculpture of two nude dancing ballerinas stirred up some controversy when it first graced Peachtree Street, but is now a familiar part of the area.

OPPOSITE PAGE: Neighborhoods in the Midtown area are known for their quaint tree-lined streets. But the district is rich with must-see places, including Piedmont Park, the Woodruff Arts Center, the Fox Theatre, the Atlanta Botanical Garden, the Carter Presidential Center, Georgia Institute of Technology, and the apartment building where Margaret Mitchell wrote much of *Gone with the Wind.*

Atlanta from the Ashes is a bronze monument located in Woodruff Park. Commonly known as *The Phoenix*, the monument symbolizes the city's rise from the ashes of the Civil War to become one of the most important cities in the world.

One of the city's first skyscrapers, the
17-story Hurt Building is made up of three
parts – a four-story base, a 13-story shaft
and a decorative cornice. Built by Atlanta
developer Joel Hurt, it is one of the oldest
skyscrapers in the country – its first tenant
occupied the building in 1913. Viewers
of the Andy Griffith television series
Matlock will recognize the exterior of
the building, which stood in for the office
of the fictional lawyer.

The architecturally striking Spire Tower condominium is located on Peachtree Street. The landmark building is in the center of the "Midtown Mile" – a district famous for shops, entertainment, parks, restaurants and cultural institutions.

The Pinnacle, a 22-story skyscraper, forms a distinctive part of the Atlanta skyline. The building is located in the Buckhead district, the financial center of the city and the Southeast.

The stainless steel sculpture *Early Mace* was created by Charles O. Perry. The patterns made by this impressive work change many times as a person walks by. The one-ton sculpture was installed in 1971 at Peachtree Center before being moved to its present location at the SunTrust Plaza.

Peachtree Road, lined with towering offices, hotels and condominiums, is the main artery of the Buckhead area. Buckhead is popular for its upscale restaurants, lively nightlife and luxury shopping. The area was established as a stagecoach stop in the mid-19th century. According to legend, the name came from a buck's head said to have hung in the bar of a local tavern.

ABOVE: Following college sports is an Atlanta tradition. At the Georgia Institute of Technology (Georgia Tech), historic Grant Field has been home to the Yellow Jackets football team – often referred to as the Ramblin' Wreck – since 1913.

LEFT: Atlanta is home to some of the country's best sports teams, top athletic facilities and most enthusiastic sports fans. The Atlanta Falcons play record-setting home games at the Georgia Dome. Other teams include Major League Baseball's Atlanta Braves, the Atlanta Hawks of the NBA, the Atlanta Dream of the WNBA, and the Atlanta Thrashers of the NHL.

This bronze statue shows Hank Aaron hitting his 715th – and Major League record – home run in April 1974. Located outside the northern entrance to Turner Field, the statue was sculpted by Ed Dwight, Jr., in 1982. The American baseball icon, nicknamed "Hammerin' Hank," is widely regarded as one of the greatest hitters in the history of the sport.

Turner Field provides the atmosphere of old-time baseball while offering modern-day comforts. After opening in 1997, the "Home of the Braves" soon became a city landmark. Originally an 80,000-seat stadium built for the Olympic Games, Turner Field now seats 50,000 spectators. Fans can visit the Braves Museum and Hall of Fame, which displays artifacts and photos that trace the team's beginnings.

Atlanta has more than a hundred public and private golf courses in its metropolitan areas. Some of these are quite spectacular and offer a welcome respite from the pace of big city life. The city is intensely proud of its golf history. The legendary Bobby Jones was born in Atlanta and attended the Georgia Institute of Technology.

OPPOSITE PAGE: The Atlanta Motor Speedway is located just outside Hampton, about 20 miles south of Atlanta. The 1.54-mile track, one of the fastest on the NASCAR circuit, opened in 1960 and has seating capacity of more than 125,000.

The Metropolitan Atlanta Rapid Transit Authority, commonly called MARTA, is among the largest and busiest rapid-transit systems in the United States. Still, many commuters rely on cars, resulting in heavy traffic. Metro Atlanta often appears at or near the top of lists of longest commute times in the country.

OPPOSITE PAGE: The Peachtree Road Race, a city-wide tradition, is a 10-kilometer race held annually on July 4th. Drawing about 55,000 runners, it has been the world's largest 10-kilometer race for more than three decades. The event also includes a wheelchair race, which precedes the footrace.

The Hartsfield-Jackson International Airport is the world's busiest – both in passengers and in number of flights. The city serves as a major hub for travel throughout the Southeastern United States and has more than 200 domestic and international gates.

Listed on the National Register of Historic Places and operated by the Atlanta History Center, the Margaret Mitchell House is a turn-of-the-century building where the author lived and wrote most of her Pulitzer Prize–winning novel, *Gone with the Wind*. Today one of the city's most popular tourist attractions, it features guided tours of the apartment where Mitchell wrote her classic book.

The Atlanta Civil War Museum and Cyclorama, located in Grant Park, is home to the largest of only three cycloramas in the United States. It also contains exhibits of Civil War arms and artillery, paintings and photographs related to the war, and the steam locomotive *Texas*. The Cyclorama painting itself (see the following pages) is augmented by a three-dimensional diorama in front of the painting and a narration of the events of the Battle of Atlanta.

The immense Cyclorama painting – 42 feet tall and 358 feet in circumference – was created in 1885–86 to immortalize the 1864 Civil War campaign of the Battle of Atlanta. Visitors view a cyclorama from the inside. The central cylinder rotates slowly, affording a view of the entire painting.

Stone Mountain Park, about 16 miles east of downtown Atlanta, is among the most popular attractions in Georgia. It is best known for the enormous carving on the northern face of the mountain – the largest such carving in the world – which depicts three Confederate leaders of the Civil War: President Jefferson Davis and Generals Thomas J. "Stonewall" Jackson and Robert E. Lee. The park presents a daily concert from its 732-bell carillon.

The Martin Luther King, Jr., birth home, at 501 Auburn Avenue, was built in 1895 and has been restored to its 1929–41 condition (when the King family lived here). The home is part of the Sweet Auburn Historic District, the neighborhood that served as the center of African American life from the 1890s to the 1940s.

REV. MARTIN LUTHER KING, JR.
1929 ~ 1968
"Free at last, Free at last,
Thank God Almighty
I'm Free at last."

CORETTA SCOTT KING
1927 ~ 2006
"And now abide Faith, Hope,
Love, These Three; but the
greatest of these is Love."
I Cor. 13:13

Visitors can pay tribute to and learn about the great civil rights leader at the King Center, where the grave site of Dr. Martin Luther King, Jr., is located. The site is administered by the National Park Service. Coretta Scott King was interred with her husband in 2006. An eternal flame is located nearby.

Ebenezer Baptist Church on Auburn Avenue is an historic landmark. From 1960 to 1968, Martin Luther King, Jr., shared the pulpit with his father. The red brick building, which was completed in 1922, was a spiritual center of the nonviolent civil rights movement. Recordings of Dr. King's sermons and speeches play inside the church, in his own voice.

The Cathedral of Christ the King is on Peachtree Road in the Buckhead area. Built in 1936 and designed in the French Gothic architectural style, the cathedral serves Atlanta's large Catholic population.

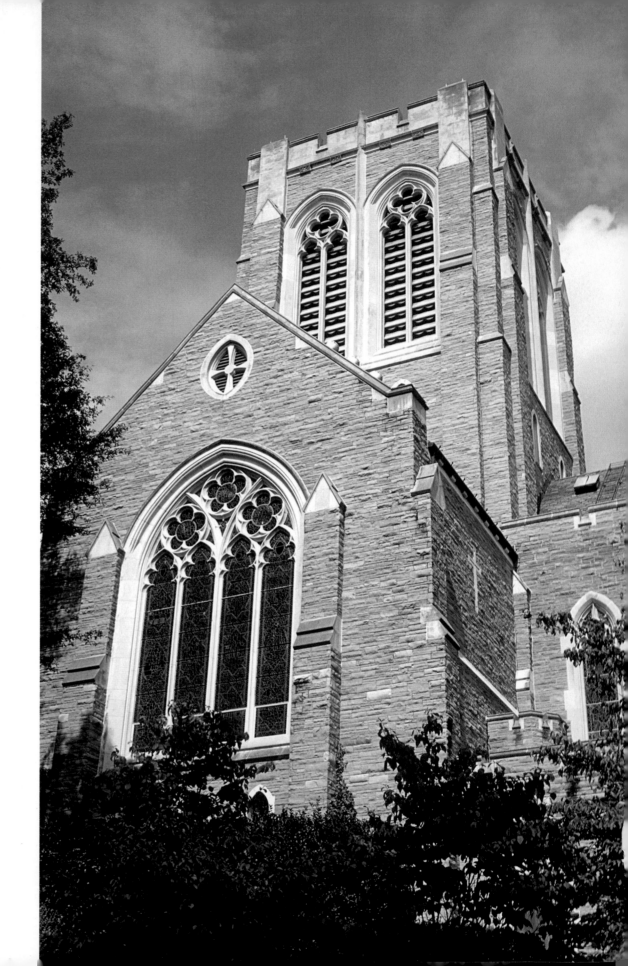

The Cathedral of St. Philip, located on Peachtree Road in the Buckhead area, is one of the largest Episcopal congregations in the country.

The Temple, located in Midtown Atlanta, has served as a center for Atlanta's Jewish cultural, educational and social activities since its construction in 1931.

The Varsity bills itself as the world's largest drive-in restaurant. It has been serving customers since 1928, and people from all over the world visit to learn about its history. The main downtown location can accommodate 600 cars and more than 800 people. Two miles of hot dogs, 300 gallons of chili, and 5,000 fried pies are made daily.

Underground Atlanta, now a retail and entertainment complex occupying 12 acres in the heart of Downtown, was a bustling district during the post–Civil War reconstruction era. Many significant features from original storefronts have survived, including granite archways and decorative brickwork. Markers pinpoint historic sites.

The Sweet Auburn Curb Market, a municipal market dating back to 1923, occupies 50,000 square feet. Known by its present name for the past two decades, the market has been recently restored. In addition to groceries and fresh produce, the market sells fully cooked regional specialties – including chitlins.

Farmers bring truckloads of produce every morning to the vast Atlanta State Farmers' Market, about 12 miles south of the city's downtown. At 150 acres, the market, which is open to the public, is considered one of the largest of its kind in the country.

The Mall of Georgia is a regional mega-mall, about 30 miles northeast of Atlanta. At 1.7 million square feet, it is the largest mall in the Southeast. About 225 stores are located here, including major department stores and many specialty shops.

The upscale Phipps Plaza is located in the city's affluent Buckhead area. It is known not only for its high-end department stores and boutiques, but also for its extravagant interior, consisting of mahogany walls, marble floors, glass elevators and a massive staircase.

As the state capital and the largest city in the Southeast, Atlanta is home to many government buildings. The National Archives at Atlanta maintains historical records of federal agencies in eight southern states, including Georgia.

OPPOSITE PAGE: The 14-story City Hall is a superb example of neo-Gothic architecture. On this site once stood the John Neal House, used by General Sherman as his headquarters following the city's surrender during the Civil War.

The Governor's Mansion is a three-floor, 30-room, Greek Revival–style home that stands on about 18 acres on historic West Paces Ferry Road in northeast Atlanta. The mansion was built in 1967 and is the official home of the governor and his family. There are 30 Doric columns, made from California redwoods, around the porches. All furnishings are of museum quality, and the mansion is open to the public at scheduled times.

The Georgia State Capitol was built to symbolize the state's re-emergence after the Civil War. An architecturally significant building, it has been named a National Historic landmark and is listed on the National Register of Historic Places. The building was completed in 1889 and designed to resemble the Classical architectural style of the US Capitol. In 1958, the dome was gilded with gold leaf from Georgia's Lumpkin County, where the first American gold rush took place. Adorning the dome is the statue *Miss Freedom*.

The Jimmy Carter Presidential Center, just east of Downtown, is home to both the Carter Center and the Jimmy Carter Presidential Library and Museum. The center was founded by the former president and his wife, Rosalynn Carter, to advance peace and health worldwide. It includes a replica of the Oval Office and traces the 39th president's life – from his sixth grade report card to his 2002 Nobel Peace Prize.

Atlanta is home to several internationally recognized institutions of higher learning. Morehouse College is an all-male, historically black college and the alma mater of many prominent African Americans, including Dr. Martin Luther King, Jr., filmmaker Spike Lee, actor Samuel L. Jackson, and Olympic gold medalist Edwin Moses. The school's origins date back to 1867, two years after the American Civil War.

OPPOSITE PAGE: Emory University is located on a beautiful campus in Atlanta's picturesque Druid Hills neighborhood. Ranked among the top schools in the country, the university offers academic degrees and programs through nine schools. The historic institution was founded by the Methodist Church in 1836. Buildings are designed in the Italian Renaissance style, with Georgia marble used in the exteriors.

The Georgia Institute of Technology is one of the country's top research universities. Its main campus occupies a large part of Midtown Atlanta. Athletics are an important part of student life. During the 1996 Olympic Games, the campus was the site of the athletes' village and a venue for a number of events.

There are a number of historic and picturesque locations outside the Atlanta area. Marietta, about 20 miles northeast of the city, offers grand antebellum homes, heritage sites and the Gone with the Wind Movie Museum. The city's Marietta Square is the local gathering place.

Roswell, about 30 miles north of Atlanta, is listed on the National Register of Historic Places. Martha Bulloch Roosevelt, mother of President Theodore Roosevelt, lived in Bulloch Hall, one of several mansions worth seeing here. The house has been preserved and restored, and is open to the public.

OPPOSITE PAGE: Lake Lanier is about 50 miles northeast of Atlanta, nestled in the foothills of the Georgia Blue Ridge Mountains. Locals and visitors enjoy the tranquility of the lake, which is popular with boaters.

Atlanta is a city of festivals. The annual Dogwood Festival at Piedmont Park takes place in early April, when the native dogwoods are in full bloom. A hot-air balloon race is a popular attraction of the event.

Piedmont Park – Atlanta's "Common Ground" – at night.

FOLLOWING PAGE: The Chattahoochee River is a natural resource that provides water, recreation and beauty for the Atlanta region. From its source in the Blue Ridge Mountains, the river flows southwesterly through Atlanta and its suburbs.